Get up and running right away with this exclusive hands-on book

Learn the basics — in under one hour!

Master hot new features quickly and easily

Microsoft FrontPage® 2000

Bible

Quick Start

Kelly Murdock

What's New in Microsoft FrontPage 2000?

- ✦ **Combined interface:** FrontPage 2000 combines the Explorer module and the Editor module into one program. This makes it easier to work with files from within one single application.

- ✦ **Dynamic HTML transitions:** FrontPage 2000 allows you to quickly add Dynamic HTML transition Effects to your Web pages. These let you make text or images respond to events such as a mouse over or a click with different effects such as a fly-in, spiral, wave, wipe, and zoom.

- ✦ **Customizable themes:** FrontPage 2000 includes 60 pre-designed themes that can make any Web site look great. These themes can now be easily modified to include personal logos and names.

- ✦ **HTML source preservation:** FrontPage 2000 will not modify the HTML source code as pages are edited. Code can be entered and formatted in the HTML View without changing the source code.

- ✦ **Database integration:** FrontPage 2000 includes support for interacting with a database via Web forms. Query results can be posted to a dynamically generated page and form data can be logged in to a database.

- ✦ **Built-in FTP publishing:** Publishing Web files can be completed from within the FrontPage environment.

- ✦ **Check in/check out:** To manage a team of Web page creators, pages can be assigned and checked out to different authors. This will keep other authors from making changes on top of current changes.

- ✦ **Better integration with Office:** All the Office products have been updated to better handle HTML output and input. This will let you work between the Office applications and FrontPage without a lot of rework.

- ✦ **No server required:** FrontPage 2000 no longer requires the Personal Web Server to be installed.

Microsoft® FrontPage® 2000 Bible Quick Start

Kelly Murdock

IDG Books Worldwide, Inc.
An International Data Group Company

Foster City, CA ✦ Chicago, IL ✦ Indianapolis, IN ✦ New York, NY

Microsoft® FrontPage® 2000 Bible Quick Start

Published by
IDG Books Worldwide, Inc.
An International Data Group Company
919 E. Hillsdale Blvd., Suite 400
Foster City, CA 94404
www.idgbooks.com (IDG Books Worldwide Web site)

Part Number: D466

Printed in the United States of America

10 9 8 7 6 5 4 3

1B/SU/QT/ZZ/FC

Distributed in the United States by IDG Books Worldwide, Inc.

Distributed by CDG Books Canada Inc. for Canada; by Transworld Publishers Limited in the United Kingdom; by IDG Norge Books for Norway; by IDG Sweden Books for Sweden; by Woodslane Pty. Ltd. for Australia; by Woodslane (NZ) Ltd. for New Zealand; by TransQuest Publishers Pte Ltd. for Singapore, Malaysia, Thailand, Indonesia, and Hong Kong; by ICG Muse, Inc. for Japan; by Norma Comunicaciones S.A. for Colombia; by Intersoft for South Africa; by Le Monde en Tique for France; by International Thomson Publishing for Germany, Austria, and Switzerland; by Distribuidora Cuspide for Argentina; by Livraria Cultura for Brazil; by Ediciones ZETA S.C.R. Ltda. for Peru; by WS Computer Publishing Corporation, Inc., for the Philippines; by Contemporanea de Ediciones for Venezuela; by Express Computer Distributors for the Caribbean and West Indies; by Micronesia Media Distributor, Inc. for Micronesia; by Grupo Editorial Norma S.A. for Guatemala; by Chips Computadoras S.A. de C.V. for Mexico; by Editorial Norma de Panama S.A. for Panama; by American Bookshops for Finland. Authorized Sales Agent: Anthony Rudkin Associates for the Middle East and North Africa.

For general information on IDG Books Worldwide's books in the U.S., please call our Consumer Customer Service department at 800-762-2974. For reseller information, including discounts and premium sales, please call our Reseller Customer Service department at 800-434-3422.

For information on where to purchase IDG Books Worldwide's books outside the U.S., please contact our International Sales department at 650-655-3200 or fax 650-655-3297.

For information on foreign language translations, please contact our Foreign & Subsidiary Rights department at 650-655-3021 or fax 650-655-3281.

For sales inquiries and special prices for bulk quantities, please contact our Sales department at 650-655-3200 or write to the address above.

For information on using IDG Books Worldwide's books in the classroom or for ordering examination copies, please contact our Educational Sales department at 800-434-2086 or fax 317-596-5499.

For press review copies, author interviews, or other publicity information, please contact our Public Relations department at 650-655-3000 or fax 650-655-3299.

For authorization to photocopy items for corporate, personal, or educational use, please contact Copyright Clearance Center, 222 Rosewood Drive, Danvers, MA 01923, or fax 978-750-4470.

Contents

Welcome to the *Microsoft FrontPage 2000 Bible Quick Start*

Thank you for picking up the *Microsoft FrontPage 2000 Bible Quick Start*. We designed this booklet to give you a quick introduction to FrontPage 2000, the latest version of the world's most popular Web page creation software.

Learning a software product is a voyage of discovery. When you are first learning a program, or just want to get an overview of the new features in the latest version of a software product, it can be time-consuming and frustrating to set sail before you even have an idea of where you're going. We created this booklet to ease you into FrontPage 2000 and to help you get up to speed on its new features quickly and with little fuss. This handy booklet will help you discover:

- ✦ **What's New:** FrontPage 2000 includes many new features and capabilities that will help you create powerful, cutting-edge Web pages. These new features are listed on the inside front cover and are highlighted with a special icon throughout the booklet, so that you can find them quickly and easily.

- ✦ **Quick Start Your Web Site:** Need a Web presence fast? Want to jump right in and do some work? The Quick Start tasks show you how to get your Web pages up in the least amount of time.

- ✦ **Top FrontPage Time-savers:** Like many programs, FrontPage 2000 has some common hang-ups that can slow you down, as well as tips that can help you work more quickly. Our expert authors share their time-saving advice.

- ✦ **Top FrontPage Design Tips:** To maximize FrontPage to create winning presentations, you need to tap into the designer in you. These tips help you to understand common design precepts.

- ✦ **Keyboard Shortcuts:** These shortcuts help you to do your work efficiently. You can fold over the back page and keep this handy section right by your computer until these shortcuts become second nature.

With its unique (and brief!) format, the *Quick Start* covers all of these items in just 32 pages. We believe that this booklet can help you gain confidence in using FrontPage 2000 in less than an hour.

How Does This Booklet Work with the *Microsoft FrontPage 2000 Bible?*

You probably discovered this booklet tucked inside the *Microsoft FrontPage 2000 Bible*. Or, perhaps a friend or colleague passed this on to you. No matter how it came into your hands, you may be wondering how this *Quick Start* works with the much-larger *Bible*.

The *Quick Start* is designed to work with the *Bible* to give you more flexibility. The *Quick Start* provides a quick overview of FrontPage 2000 and its features. You can also get your feet wet by working through an initial presentation, and by learning some handy time-savers, design tips, and keyboard shortcuts. In addition, the *Quick Start* is designed to go anywhere with you. It will fit in a briefcase for quick access, and will get you started when you need answers in a hurry. If you haven't used FrontPage in a while, it will also jog your memory on the skills that you've already mastered.

As you can tell by its much larger size, the *Bible* dives very deep into FrontPage and provides not only coverage of the same skills overviewed in this booklet, but 100 percent of the material that you need to learn and master the program. Expert author Joe Smith covers every feature and capability of FrontPage 2000 and shows you how to make them work for you. The book includes loads of advice, hundreds of tips, rich example presentations, and a CD-ROM containing useful shareware. In general, the *Bible* provides the background, real-world examples, and depth of coverage that you need to become a FrontPage power user.

For More Information

After you get your feet wet using the *Quick Start*, you will probably want to learn how to maximize the power of FrontPage 2000. As previously noted, the *Microsoft FrontPage 2000 Bible* is a strong all-in-one reference that will help you master the program. If you don't already have the *Bible*, you can order it by following the instructions in the back of the *Quick Start*.

For those who prefer a different learning style, IDG Books Worldwide has more to offer. Please take a look at our new *Teach Yourself Microsoft FrontPage 2000*, which provides a visual, hands-on approach to learning. You can order this title by following the instructions in the back of the *Quick Start*.

Contact Us!

We hope that you find this *Quick Start* useful. We are always looking for ways to make our books better, and your feedback is very important to us. Please let us know what you think. You can contact us by any of the following ways:

✦ Contact us through our Web site: www.idgbooks.com

✦ Send mail to us: IDG Books Worldwide, Inc. ATTN: Customer Service, 7260 Shadeland Station, Indianapolis, IN 46256

✦ Call us: 800-762-2974

Building Basic Web Pages

When you start FrontPage (Start ➪ Programs ➪ Microsoft FrontPage), you'll first notice that it launches straight into Page view mode, with a blank page ready for you to work with, much like Word or Excel. This page-centric approach is a major new focus for FrontPage 2000, making the application act and look much like the other Office products.

Page view is where you'll spend most of your time in FrontPage, but other ways to view your progress are included. The View bar is also visible when you first start FrontPage. This bar lets you look at your development in different ways. If the View bar isn't visible, you can open it by selecting View ➪ View Bar. Figure 1-1 shows the View bar, which includes the following views:

- **Page view:** A WYSIWYG view of the current page.
- **Folders view:** A snapshot of all your files, presented just like Explorer would show them.
- **Reports view:** Reports can be generated to show you details such as broken links and which pages load slowly.
- **Navigation view:** A view of all the pages in a Web and the links between them.
- **Hyperlinks view:** Shows all the links between pages.
- **Tasks view:** Helps you to keep track of who is doing what, and what needs to be completed.

The first development that you likely will to want to do is to start building Web pages. This first section focuses on building basic Web pages.

New Feature FrontPage provides an integrated interface, which makes it easy to starting building a Web page.

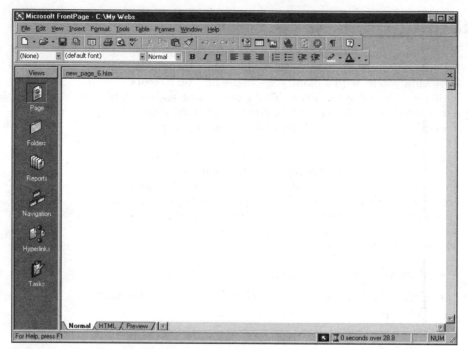

Figure 1-1: Starting FrontPage shows the View bar. You can turn off the View bar by selecting View ➪ View Bar.

Creating a new Web page

Before you create a Web site, you need to create individual pages. FrontPage includes several templates and wizards to get your started. You can get an idea of what a page will look like by clicking the page and looking at the Preview section.

To create a new Web page, follow these steps:

1. Select File ➪ New ➪ Page, or press Ctrl+N. This opens the New dialog box (Figure 1-2), which includes several templates and wizards, shown as icons.

2. Select a template and click the OK button.

3. The new page opens with dummy text and graphics that you can easily replace.

Note   The wizards and style sheet templates are unavailable to preview from within the New dialog box.

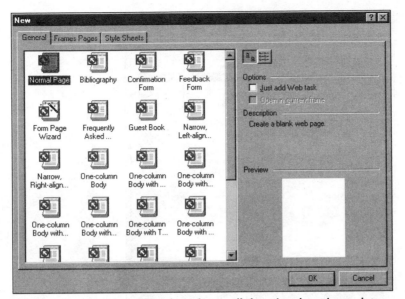

Figure 1-2: The New dialog box shows all the wizards and templates as icons.

Adding and formatting text

Perhaps the easiest content to add to a Web page is text. Text is added simply by typing. Adding text to a Web page should feel very similar to using Word. Many of the formatting features and menus are identical to Word. If you have text in Word, you can use the copy-and-paste features, or even drag and drop the text from Word to FrontPage.

To format FrontPage text, follow these steps:

1. Select the text to modify either by dragging the mouse over a section of text or by double-clicking a single word.

2. Make sure the Formatting toolbar is visible, by selecting View ⇨ Toolbars ⇨ Formatting.

3. Click the icon of the formatting option that you want. For example, clicking the B icon causes the selected text to be bold.

4. Another way to apply formatting to the selected text is with the Format menus. For example, selecting Format ⇨ Font opens the Font dialog box (Figure 1-3), in which several formatting options can be selected and applied simultaneously.

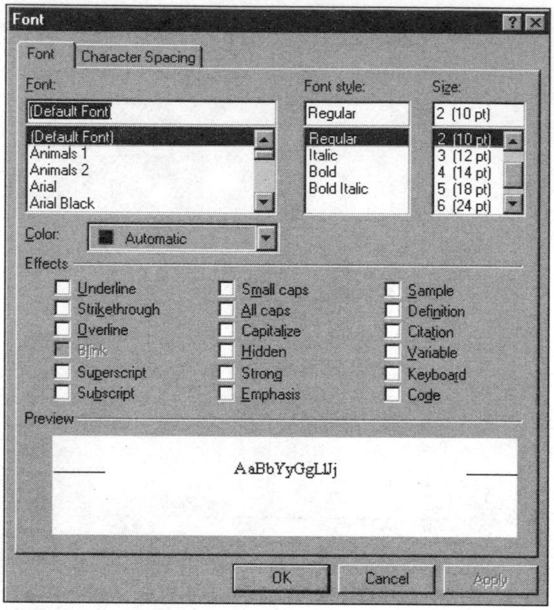

Figure 1-3: The Font dialog box enables you to edit how your text looks.

5. Select the formatting options and apply them by clicking the OK button.

Note

The Font dialog box includes several formatting effects native to HTML that are not included on the Formatting toolbar, such as strikethrough, subscript, superscript, and strong.

The Format menu includes dialog boxes for the following:

✦ **Font:** Defines the font, style, size, text color, effects, and spacing.

✦ **Paragraph:** Defines the alignment, indentation, and paragraph spacing.

✦ **Bullets and Numbering:** Defines the bullet types, number types, and starting value.

✦ **Borders and Shading:** Defines the border style, colors, padding, and shading values.

✦ **Position:** Defines the wrapping and positioning styles and locations.

Placing text in lists

FrontPage has two basic types of lists in common with Word. HTML has a third type, known as a *definition list*. Every other line of a definition list is indented, as if you were including a definition for the word indented under each word in the list.

To create a list, follow these steps:

1. Select the text that you want to make into a list by dragging the mouse over the list contents. Each separate paragraph of text becomes an entry in the list.

2. Make sure the Formatting toolbar is visible, by selecting View ➪ Toolbars ➪ Formatting.

3. Click the Numbering icon to create a numbered list, or click the Bullets icon to create a bulleted list. To create a definition list, click the Style drop-down list to the far left of the Formatting toolbar and then select Definition.

Note
Headings are commonly used in Web pages. To create headings, labeled in size from 1 (largest) to 6 (smallest), select the text and then select a heading size from the Style drop-down list on the far left of the Formatting toolbar.

4. Another way to create a list is with the Format ➪ Bullets and Numbering menu. This opens the List Properties dialog box, in which you can change the type of bullet, change the type of number, load a different bullet graphic, or change the starting number.

5. After the list is created, the List Properties dialog box can be easily accessed by right-clicking an item in the list and selecting List Properties from the pop-up menu.

Inserting special characters

The keyboard includes most, but not all, of the characters that make up the text that you'll want to include in your Web pages. Occasionally, you'll want to include a special character, such as a copyright or trademark symbol.

To add a special character or symbol, follow these steps:

1. Position the cursor at the location where you want to insert the symbol.

2. Click the Insert ➪ Symbol menu. This brings up the Symbol dialog box (Figure 1-4), in which you can select the symbol that you want to use.

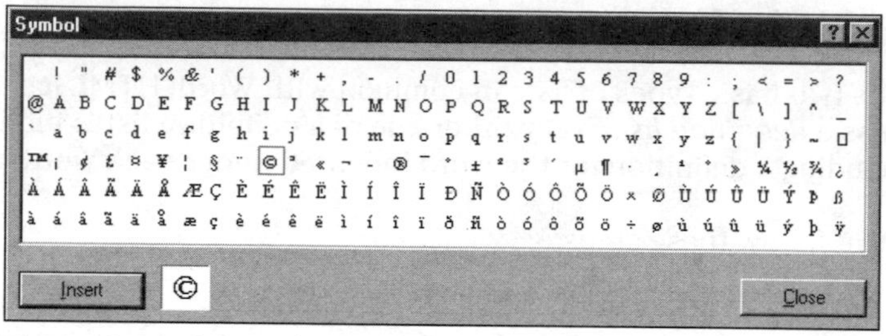

Figure 1-4: The Symbol dialog box enables you to insert several symbols simultaneously.

3. Select the symbol that you want to use. An enlarged view of the symbol is shown at the bottom of the dialog box.

4. Click the Insert button to insert the symbol. To insert another symbol, select another symbol and click Insert again.

5. When you're finished inserting symbols, close the dialog box by clicking the Close button.

Accessing the Page Properties dialog box

The Page Properties dialog box is where you set the default settings for the individual page. The properties are divided into four tabs:

+ **General:** Page locations, title, target frame, background sound, and scripting types.

+ **Background:** Background pictures, watermarks, rollover effects, and link colors.

+ **Custom:** System and user variables.

+ **Language:** Page language settings.

To open the Page Properties dialog box, follow these steps:

1. Right-click anywhere on the page and select Page Properties from the pop-up menu. This opens the Page Properties dialog box, shown in Figure 1-5.

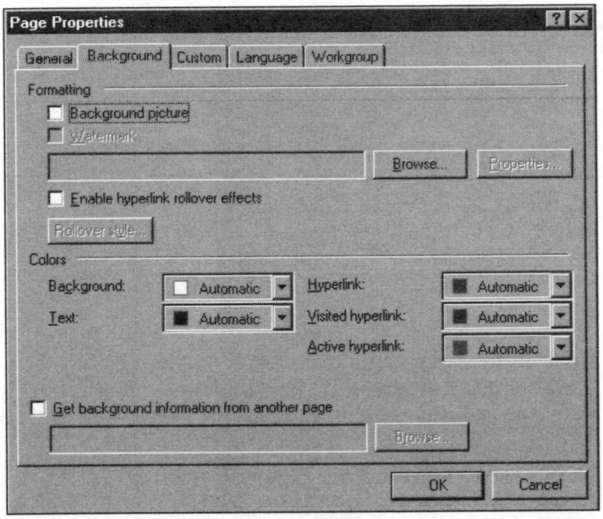

Figure 1-5: The Page Properties dialog box includes several different tabs for controlling many aspects of the page.

2. Click the Background tab.

3. Under Colors, select a new color from the Background color pull-down menu.

4. Click OK, and the color is applied to the background of the page.

Creating hyperlinks and bookmarks

Hyperlinks are markings that allow text on one Web page to load another page when clicked. Hyperlinks don't need to be just text, either. Images can also be hyperlinks. A *bookmark* is similar to a hyperlink, except that it connects to a different location within the same Web page. Bookmarks are useful for creating jump lists at the top of a page.

Create and use hyperlinks and bookmarks by following these steps:

1. Select the text that you want to make into a hyperlink or bookmark by dragging the mouse over a section of text or by double-clicking a single word.

2. Make sure the Standard toolbar is visible, by selecting View ⇨ Toolbars ⇨ Standard.

3. Click the Hyperlink icon. It looks like a blue globe with a chain link underneath. This brings up the Create Hyperlink dialog box, shown in Figure 1-6.

4. Within the Create Hyperlink dialog box is a list of pages included in the current Web. You can link to these pages by selecting a page from the list and clicking OK.

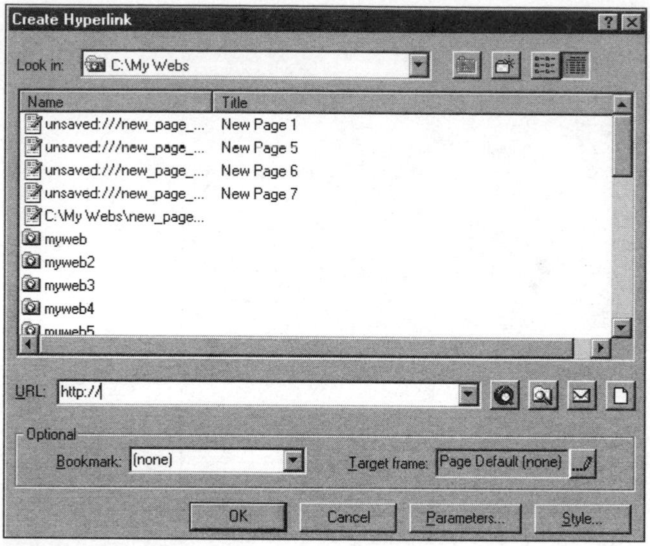

Figure 1-6: The Create Hyperlink dialog box provides several ways to locate hyperlinks.

5. Another option is to type the URL or address of the page on the World Wide Web. Perhaps an easier way to link to pages on the Web is to click the icon to the immediate right of the URL text field. This enables you to locate the page by using your browser.

6. The other icons let you link to a local file, create a link that sends e-mail, or link to a new page that hasn't been built yet.

7. By using the Create Hyperlink dialog box, you can also link to bookmarks set up with the page. To create a bookmark, select some text, choose Insert ⇨ Bookmark, and then give the bookmark a name. After you create a bookmark, it appears in the Create Hyperlink dialog box, where you can link to it by selecting it and clicking OK.

Note

You can quickly test any hyperlinks by holding down the Ctrl key and clicking the hyperlink. Also, as you scroll over a hyperlink, the link's address appears in the status bar at the bottom of the window.

Adding images

A Web page without images can be pretty boring. Images can enliven a Web page, if used correctly. Web pages use images saved in one of three formats: GIF, JPEG, or PNG. Each of these file types has advantages and disadvantages. Although Web pages can use these three formats only, FrontPage can load many different types of image formats, including BMP, WMF, TIF, EPS, and TGA. When you save a page containing one of these types, FrontPage prompts you to save the images in GIF, JPG, or PNG format.

Add images to a Web page by following these steps:

1. Position the cursor at the location where you want to insert the image.

2. Click Insert ⇨ Picture ⇨ From File. This brings up the Picture dialog box (Figure 1-7), where you can select the image that you want to load.

3. If you don't have an image to load, you can select Insert ⇨ Picture ⇨ Clip Art to access the clip art library.

4. Another way to add an image is by clicking the Picture icon in the Standard toolbar.

5. In the Picture dialog box, you are given a list of images for the current Web, or you can enter the URL for an image somewhere on the World Wide Web.

6. When you select an image file, the area to the right displays a preview of the graphic. If this is the image that you want to load, click the OK button, and the image appears on the page.

7. To change any of the image settings, right-click the image and select Picture Properties from the pop-up menu. Within the Picture Properties dialog box (Figure 1-8), you can change the picture source, image type, alternate text, hyperlinks, alignment, border width, spacing, and image size. Click OK to apply any changes.

Figure 1-7: The Picture dialog box lets you preview images before loading them.

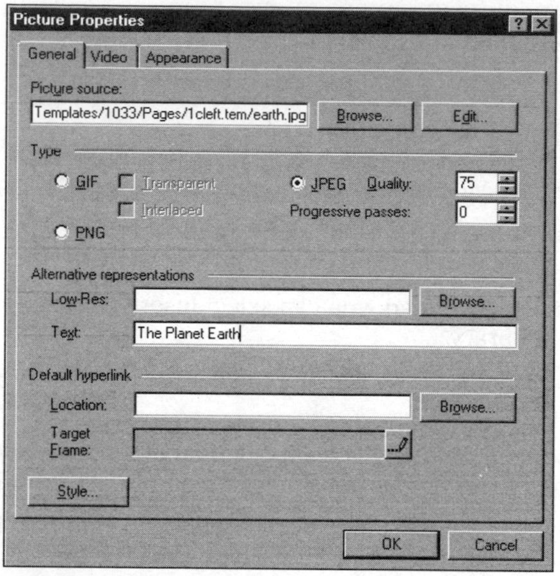

Figure 1-8: The Picture Properties dialog box includes General, Video, and Appearance tabs.

Scanning images into FrontPage

FrontPage also has the functionality to scan images directly into a Web page. This feature saves the trouble of using scanner software to scan and save images just so that they can be loaded into FrontPage. This method can also be used for digital cameras.

To scan an image into FrontPage, follow these steps:

1. Position the cursor at the location where you want to insert the scanned image.

2. Click the Picture icon in the Standard toolbar.

3. When the Picture dialog box comes up, click the Scan button. You need to have a scanner or digital camera properly connected and configured to your computer.

4. The Camera/Scanner dialog box appears. To select the scanner driver, click the Source button and choose the driver that you want to use.

5. Click the Acquire button to retrieve the image from your scanner or digital camera.

6. When the scanning process is complete, close the Camera/Scanner dialog box by clicking the Close button.

Editing images within FrontPage

FrontPage includes several basic image-editing options that don't require help from an additional graphics package. Although you probably won't be using FrontPage to create your images, you can use it to perform some basic editing. These editing features can be found on the Picture toolbar that appears any time that an image is selected.

Note You can make the Picture toolbar appear at any time by selecting View ➪ Toolbars ➪ Picture. But, if an image isn't selected, most of the buttons on the Picture toolbar are disabled.

The Picture buttons are grouped into six different sections:

✦ Special Features Group (Text, Auto Thumbnail)

✦ Position Group (Absolutely Positioned, Bring to Front, Send to Back)

✦ Rotation Group (Rotate Left, Rotate Right, Flip Vertical, Flip Horizontal)

✦ Contrast and Brightness Group (More Contrast, Less Contrast, More Brightness, Less Brightness)

✦ Image Altering Group (Crop, Set Transparent Color, Black and White, Wash Out, Bevel, Resample)

✦ Hotspot Group (Select, Rectangular Hotspot, Circular Hotspot, Polygonal Hotspot, Highlight Hotspots)

Creating Auto Thumbnails

A Web page with many large images can take a long time to display. Thumbnails are small versions of the large image, with links to the actual image. FrontPage's Auto Thumbnail feature creates these thumbnails and links automatically.

To create Auto Thumbnails, follow these steps:

1. Select the image or images that you want to convert into a thumbnail. When you select an image, the Picture toolbar, shown in Figure 1-9, automatically appears at the bottom of the window.

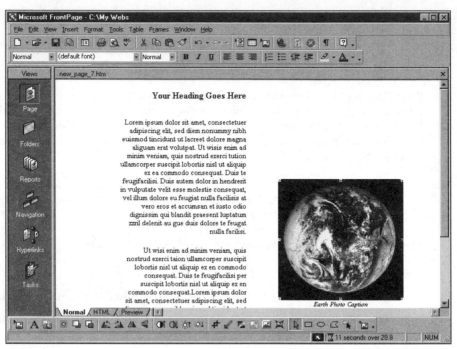

Figure 1-9: Most icons on the Picture toolbar are applied immediately.

2. Click the Auto Thumbnail icon in the Picture toolbar. This icon is the third from the left.

3. The image size is automatically reduced to the size specified in the Page Options dialog box. You can change the default thumbnail size by selecting Tools ⇨ Page Options and clicking the Auto Thumbnail tab.

Note The Page Options dialog box includes many useful default settings that effect the page elements. Other tabs in the Page Options dialog box include: General, Default Font, HTML Source, Color Coding, Spelling, and Compatibility.

Building image maps

Images that include several links are called *image maps* and they are easy to create by using FrontPage. To create an image map, you need to define areas called *hotspots*, and assign a link. These hotspots can be circular, rectangular, or polygonal. FrontPage allows you to create these hotspots simply by drawing on an image.

To create an image map, follow these steps:

1. Make the image active by clicking it. The Picture toolbar appears.

2. Click one of the Hotspot icons at the right end of the toolbar. The options include Rectangular, Circular, and Polygonal.

3. Click and drag the mouse within the image to create a hotspot. The Create Hyperlink dialog box appears.

4. Within the Create Hyperlink dialog box, enter the URL or bookmark for the link.

5. Click the OK button to complete the link.

6. You can add additional hotspots as needed.

Caution   It is best not to overlap hotspots.

Creating a basic table

Unquestionably, Excel is the best Office tool for creating tables. Tables created in Excel can be copied and pasted or dragged and dropped into FrontPage. FrontPage also includes table-creation tools, which are similar to the tools found in Word. FrontPage includes a couple of different ways to create tables.

To create a table, follow these steps:

1. Position the cursor at the location where you want to insert the table.

2. Select Table ⇨ Insert ⇨ Table, which opens the Insert Table dialog box, shown in Figure 1-10.

3. Enter the table size by typing in the number of rows and the number of columns. You can also specify the alignment, border width, cell spacing, cell padding, and table width. After you enter the values for your table, click the OK button.

4. Another way to create a table is to click the Table icon in the Standard toolbar. This opens a fly-out grid in which you can drag the mouse over the number of cells for the table, similar to creating tables in Word.

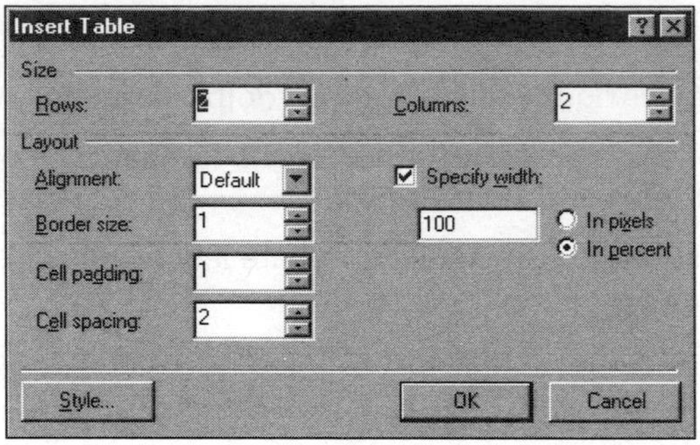

Figure 1-10: The Insert Table dialog box enables you to define many table properties before you create the table.

5. A third way to create tables is to use the Draw Table tool. Select this tool by clicking Table ➪ Draw Table. This opens the Table toolbar and puts the interface in Draw Table mode.

6. In Draw Table mode, the cursor looks like a pencil. Create the table outline by clicking and dragging the cursor to the width and height that you want for the table.

7. Additional rows and columns can be created simply by drawing them inside the outline.

8. You can modify the table by using the tools included on the Table toolbar. Tools include: draw table, eraser, insert row, insert column, delete cells, merge cells, split cells, alignment, colors, distribute evenly, and Autofit.

9. Turn off Draw Table mode either by clicking the Draw Table icon in the Table toolbar or by selecting Table ➪ Draw Table again.

After you complete the table, you can fill it with data or images by clicking in each cell and entering the data. The Tab key moves you to the next cell.

Building a form

Forms are basic Web page structures that allow the user to enter information. This information can then be saved in a file, or passed to an e-mail address. Form elements include text fields, radio buttons, check boxes, pull-down lists, and buttons.

To create a form and add form elements, follow these steps:

1. Position the cursor at the location where you want to insert the form.

2. Select Insert ➪ Form ➪ Form. This creates a form on the Web page. The form looks like a dotted rectangle and includes Submit and Reset buttons. The dotted lines are not visible when the form is viewed in a browser.

3. You can modify the form's properties by right-clicking the form and selecting Form Properties. This shows the Form Properties dialog box, in which you can change the properties, such as where to store the data and what the form is named.

4. Position the cursor within the dotted outline of the form where you want a form element to be placed.

5. Select Insert ⇨ Form ⇨ One-Line Text Box. This places a single text box at the cursor location within the form, as shown in Figure 1-11. Right-clicking each form element enables you to access the Properties dialog box for the form element.

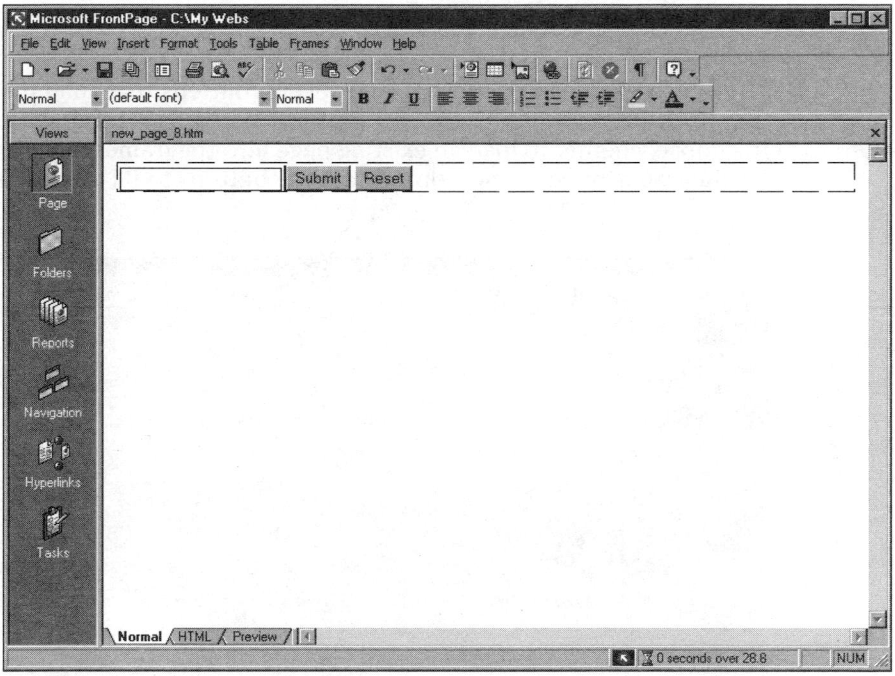

Figure 1-11: After adding a form to a page, you can include text within the form.

6. Add other form elements as needed.

7. After you complete the form, make sure that you specify what to do with the form data when the Submit button is clicked. For example, right-click the form and select Form Properties.

8. In the Form Properties dialog box, select Send to, type your e-mail address in the Email Address text field, and then click OK. This causes the form data to be sent to your e-mail mailbox when the Submit button is clicked.

Creating a new framed page

Framed pages divide the browser area into two or more sections. Individual Web pages can be placed within each of these sections. The page that divides the browser into sections is called a *frameset*, and the individual pages are called *frames*. Frames are useful when you have a page that you want displayed all the time, such as an index, with another section that shows the actual data.

To create a framed page, follow these steps:

1. Select File ⇨ New ⇨ Page to open the New dialog box.

2. Click the Frames Pages tab.

3. Select a framed template that is similar to the page that you want to create, and click OK.

4. The new framed page is created, and several buttons that span the width of the window are visible. These long buttons, shown in Figure 1-12, enables you to choose whether to load an existing page into the frame, create a new page for the frame, or get some help. Click these buttons to fill the frameset.

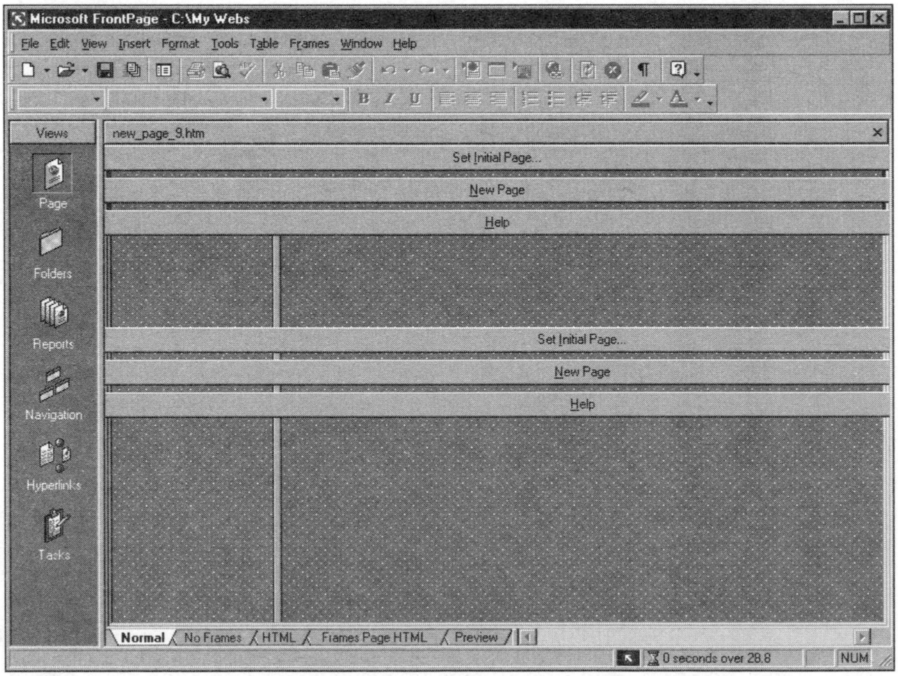

Figure 1-12: Simply click the buttons to load frames into a framed page.

5. You can resize the frames by dragging the frame borders.

6. After you fill the frames with Web pages, you can alter the frame properties by right-clicking within the frame and selecting Frame Properties.

7. The Frame Properties dialog box enables you to specify the frame name, page, size, margins, and whether the frame is resizable and has scroll bars. Click OK to apply the changes.

8. When you work with frames, the Frames menu becomes active. These menu options enable you to split frames, delete frames, or save individual frames.

Note

When you use frames, two additional tabs show up at the bottom of the Page view window. These new tabs are for viewing the No Frames option (for browsers that don't support frames) and for viewing the Frames HTML.

Configuring external editing tools

Although FrontPage includes many editing tools, sometimes you'll want to edit elements by using an external tool. FrontPage can create links to these external tools, so that when you click the element, the external tool is launched, with the element ready to be edited.

To configure external editing tools, follow these steps:

1. Select Tools ➪ Options to open the Options dialog box (Figure 1-13). Click the Configure Editors tab.

Figure 1-13: The Options dialog box includes a tab for configuring external editors.

2. Select from the list the type of page to assign to an external tool, and then click the Modify button. Or, you can add a new type by clicking the New button.

3. Type the editor's name, browse to its location, and then click OK.

4. FrontPage will now open all types using the defined external editor when double-clicked.

Publishing Your Web Pages

After you're comfortable with the pages that you've developed, you need to publish them to the Internet. This is easily accomplished with the Web Publishing Wizard.

Adding an item to the Task List

The Task List is a list of items to complete before your Web is ready to publish.

To add an item to the Task List, follow these steps:

1. Select Edit ⇨ Task ⇨ New Task, which opens the New Task dialog box. In this dialog box, you can set the name, priority, description, and the assignee.

2. You can view all the current tasks by clicking the Task view.

3. To start a task, click Edit ⇨ Task ⇨ Start.

4. After you complete the task, mark it as completed by selecting Edit ⇨ Task ⇨ Mark as Completed.

Spell Checking the Entire Web

Spelling mistakes on your Web pages detract from the polished look of a site. FrontPage enables you to spell check all the text on a single page or the entire Web. FrontPage also includes background spell checking, similar to Word.

To spell check the entire Web, follow these steps:

1. Open the Spelling dialog box by selecting Tools ⇨ Spelling.

2. Within the Spelling dialog box, you can select to spell check the current page or the entire Web.

3. After you make a selection, click the Start button to begin the spell check.

4. Spell check returns a list of misspellings. Double-click the list items to open in Page view the page containing the misspelling, which enables you to correct the mistake.

Fixing Broken Links

Few things are worse for Web visitors than finding a broken link. FrontPage offers a way to automatically verify all the links in your Web.

To fix broken links, follow these steps:

1. Find all the broken links within your Web by selecting Reports view and choosing Broken Links in the Reports toolbar. This generates a list of all the broken links.

2. If the status of any of the hyperlinks is unknown (marked with a question mark), then you can verify the links by clicking the Verify Hyperlinks button in the Reports toolbar.

3. Double-click any of the links in the list, which opens the Edit Hyperlink dialog box.

4. In this dialog box, you can change the hyperlink and click Replace.

5. In some cases, you can use the Tools ➪ Recalculate Hyperlinks feature to repair Navigation Bar links.

Publishing the Web

After you polish your pages, run spell check, and fix all the broken links, and feel ready to send your Web out to the World Wide Web, the last step is to publish.

To publish your Web to the World Wide Web, follow these steps:

1. Select File ➪ Publish Web, which opens the relatively simple Publish Web dialog box (Figure 1-14). Simply select the HTTP address where you're locating the Web, and then click Publish. You need to be connected to the Internet, of course.

Figure 1-14: The Publish Web dialog box can be expanded by clicking the Options button.

2. If you don't have a Web Publishing Provider, click the WPP's button to receive Microsoft's offer of a solution.

3. By clicking the Options button, you can access some additional features, such as publishing only the pages that have changed and requiring a secure connection.

FrontPage Top Time-savers

FrontPage is full of time-saving tools. This top ten list includes my personal favorites. As you use FrontPage, I'm sure that you'll find your own favorites.

Right-click page elements

You can right-click any Web page element to access a dynamic menu of items that pertain to that element. This right-click feature works throughout FrontPage and provides easy access to the menus that you are likely to need.

Use Hover Buttons

Creating graphical buttons can require an external graphics program and some extra time. The Hover Buttons component lets you create a variety of buttons with special effects and the ability to include sounds.

Use Auto Thumbnails

Manipulating images to reduce load time can be a tricky task. The Auto Thumbnail feature makes it easy to create a gallery of images with reasonable load times.

Spell check the entire Web

Don't get caught with misspelled words on your Web pages. If you're not a good speller, and even if you are, get in the habit of running the spell checker before publishing any new material.

Use Themes

Microsoft has included the work of many talented Web designers in its Themes. Take advantage of their work. Themes make it easy to update the look of your site instantly.

Use Shared Borders

If you're looking for consistency in your design, Shared Borders are a good place to start. By using Page Banners and Navigation Bars, much of the work is completed automatically.

Check for broken links

Another critical check before publishing is to check for broken links. This simple check will save a lot of misery for you and your visitors.

FrontPage Top Design Tips

With millions of Web pages on the Internet, good design is important if you want to get visitors to view your site. The following are some simple suggestions for designing your Web pages.

Avoid small fonts

No one likes to have to grab their reading glasses to read your content, and likely won't do so. Use font sizes that are large enough to read from a normal sitting distance.

Don't overuse frames

Many Web users don't like frames because of the area they take up, but frames can be effective if used correctly. Don't use frames unless the information contained within the frames are useful to the visitor at all times.

Use strong contrast between background and text

No one likes to read gray text on a white background. Be sensitive to your visitors by maintaining a strong contrast between your text and the background.

Use white space with all graphics

When placing images on your Web pages, don't leave your spacing values set to zero. Space between images and adjacent text gives the reader some room to breath, and leads their eyes easier between elements.

Avoid busy background graphics

A noisy background graphic can make reading the text on the page very difficult. Instead, use softer, lighter graphics that make the text easy to read.

Use matching colors

Avoid using color schemes that don't match. The Themes can provide some good insight into matching colors.

Avoid changing fonts and text colors

Page authors that use a different font or color for every paragraph make their visitors suffer. It is hard to look at too many font and color changes.

Organize data with tables and lists

Long paragraphs of text are difficult to read online. Make frequent use of tables and lists to break up your text into readable segments.

Keep your pages simple

Including too many graphics, a video, and several controls on a single page not only causes a long download, but also alienates your visitors, who will feel bombarded by too much. Instead, add more pages and spread the content around.

Don't use technologies just because you can

You should have a really good reason to use video on your Web page. Many videos can be represented sufficiently by several images. Don't use potentially confusing technologies just because it's possible.

✦   ✦   ✦

For every level, for every learning style...
IDG Books Worldwide has you covered!

SERIES	USER LEVEL	MAIN FEATURES OF SERIES	TOPICS	PAGE COUNT*
...FOR DUMMIES®	Beginning to intermediate	**...For Dummies Series** • Practical, fun, and easy-to-use books that cover topics with humor and entertainment • Filled with simple explanations, helpful icons, and clear, on-the-mark cartoons	Hundreds of computer-related books and over 100 other how-to books, covering topics from business to fitness to self-help	384–504
...FOR DUMMIES® QUICK REFERENCE	Beginning to advanced	**...For Dummies Quick Reference Series** • Pocket-size guide that offers easy-to-follow advice and easy-to-use steps for executing a program • Lay-flat, comb binding and small trim size for easy "in and out" access to software or technology features	Windows, Mac, Internet, word-processing, databases, spread-sheets, HTML, programming	220
MORE ...FOR DUMMIES®	Beginning to intermediate	**MORE ...For Dummies Series** • Starting where ...For Dummies books leave off, with more depth and breadth of topic coverage • Filled with simple explanations, helpful icons, and clear, on-the-mark cartoons	Windows, Internet, wordpro-cessing, databases, spread-sheets, suites, programming	420
DUMMIES 101®	Beginning to intermediate	**Dummies 101 Series** • Easy-to-follow tutorial with step-by-step lessons that take readers to a level of basic competency • Interactive CD-ROM with ready-to-use templates	Windows, Internet, HTML, word-processing, spreadsheets, data-bases, suites, programming	288
SMALL BUSINESS ...FOR DUMMIES®	Beginning to experienced small business technology implementers	**Small Business ...For Dummies Series** • Shows small business owners/employees how to apply technology to everyday small business situations • Filled with helpful icons and "what it means to your business" explanations • CD-ROMs with tools and applications for small businesses	Windows, networking, suites, Internet	325–400
CERTIFICATION FOR DUMMIES®	Intermediate to advanced software professionals	**Certification For Dummies Series** • Fast, focused, fun and easy reference guides that help candi-dates hone in on exam objectives and maximize study time • Written and reviewed by certified industry experts • CD-ROMs with exclusive QuickLearn™ game and Dummies test engine	Microsoft MCSE, A+ Certification	500
ONE STEP AT A TIME™	Beginning to intermediate	**One Step at a Time Series** • Book/CD-ROM combo with step-by-step, self-paced lessons • On-screen lessons with three levels of interactivity • Landscape 9" x 8" trim size and lay-flat binding • Interactive, sound-enhanced software	Office applications, Windows, Internet Explorer, graphics	350+
...SIMPLIFIED™	Beginning	**...Simplified Series** • Exclusive award-winning 3-D Visual® learning system • Full-color illustrations and screenshots • Friendly, animated disk characters who explain terms and topics simply	Office applications, Windows, Internet, HTML, hardware, America Online	200–350
TEACH YOURSELF VISUALLY™	Beginning to intermediate	**Teach Yourself VISUALLY Series** • Exclusive award-winning 3-D Visual® learning system • Full-color graphics on every page • Step-by-step, clear, concise instructions	Windows, Internet, hardware, Access, Office, Netscape Navigator, Networking, Word	350

Series	Level	Description	Topics	Page count*
MASTER VISUALLY™	Beginning to advanced	**Master VISUALLY Series** • Comprehensive reference/tutorial featuring the exclusive, award-winning 3-D Visual™ learning system • Annotated, 2-color screenshots on every page • Searchable version of book on CD-ROM	Windows 95, Windows 98, Office 97, Photoshop	704–800
TEACH YOURSELF®	Beginning to intermediate	**Teach Yourself Series** • Task-by-task organization that allows readers to take control of their learning and solve more problems in less time • Personal Workbooks with practice and Q&As • CD-ROM included with higher-end programming and networking titles	Windows, Internet, Office applications, networking, hardware, graphics	400–600
MIS: PRESS®	Beginning to advanced	**MIS: Press** • For do-it-yourself computer users who need solutions to hardware and software problems • Comprehensive and clear hands-on guides that allow readers to address and solve problems associated with PC repair and upgrade, Internet sound, AOL, and Windows 98 Registry	Upgrade & repair, Windows Registry, TCP/IP, IRQ/DMA/IO, troubleshooting PCs	400–1,000
BIBLE	Beginning to advanced	**Bible Series** • 100% authoritative, comprehensive, solution-filled reference/tutorial by an expert author or authoring team • Icons, tables, charts, and step-by-step guidelines • CD-ROM with software selected by author(s)	Windows, Mac, graphics, word-processing, NT, spreadsheets, databases, suites, programming, Internet, hardware	600–1,300
IN PLAIN ENGLISH	Beginning to advanced	**In Plain English Series** • An essential quick reference for technically savvy readers • Extensive cross-references that provide instant access to all commands in a given area • Comprehensive list of key words and commands that provide easily understood descriptions of core functions	Traditional programming and scripting languages, operating system	500–600
...SECRETS®	Intermediate to advanced	**...Secrets Series** • Filled with time-saving, undocumented tips and techniques only the pros know • CD-ROM packed with useful tools and utilities selected by the author(s)	Windows, Mac, graphics, suites, databases, programming, spreadsheets, NT, HTML, Internet	700–1,200
...STUDIO SECRETS™	Intermediate to advanced	**...Studio Secrets Series** • Lavishly illustrated, full-color interior and a unique, oversized trim size • Interviews with the experts; undocumented tips and techniques • CD-ROM with images, artwork, audio, video, and product demos	Photoshop, Illustrator, Painter, Kai's Power Tools, Web design	224+
NOVELL PRESS™	Intermediate to advanced professionals	**Novell Press Series** • Expert Novell-certified authors • Covers test prep for CNE and CNA • The only series authorized and approved by Novell, Inc.	Certification study guides, administrator handbooks, networking resources	400–1,600
ACE IT!™	Intermediate to advanced	**Ace It! Series** • Written by Microsoft exam experts who provide the inside scoop on the exam itself • Pre-/posttests, tips, quizzes, exam prep notes, and test-trap warnings that help readers make the most of their study time	Study guides, test prep for MCSE and MCSD	350–450
CERTIFICATION STUDY GUIDES	Intermediate to advanced	**Certification Study Guides Series** • Comprehensive Microsoft-approved study guides and on-the-job references • Case studies and sample exam questions • Real-world problems • Expert Microsoft-certified authors	Study guides, test prep for MCSE and MCSD	400–1,600

*approximate page count

THREE NEW SERIES COMING SOON... HEWLETT-PACKARD PRESS, ADMINISTRATOR'S HANDBOOKS, AND MASTER REFERENCES

For more information about IDG Books Worldwide's series, visit your local book retailer or log on to our Web sites www.idgbooks.com or www.dummies.com

my2cents.idgbooks.com

Register This Book — And Win!

Visit **http://my2cents.idgbooks.com** to register this book and we'll automatically enter you in our fantastic monthly prize giveaway. It's also your opportunity to give us feedback: let us know what you thought of this book and how you would like to see other topics covered.

Discover IDG Books Online!

The IDG Books Online Web site is your online resource for tackling technology — at home and at the office. Frequently updated, the IDG Books Online Web site features exclusive software, insider information, online books, and live events!

10 Productive & Career-Enhancing Things You Can Do at www.idgbooks.com

- Nab source code for your own programming projects.
- Download software.
- Read Web exclusives: special articles and book excerpts by IDG Books Worldwide authors.
- Take advantage of resources to help you advance your career as a Novell or Microsoft professional.
- Buy IDG Books Worldwide titles or find a convenient bookstore that carries them.
- Register your book and win a prize.
- Chat live online with authors.
- Sign up for regular e-mail updates about our latest books.
- Suggest a book you'd like to read or write.
- Give us your 2¢ about our books and about our Web site.

You say you're not on the Web yet? It's easy to get started with IDG Books' *Discover the Internet,* available at local retailers everywhere.

Microsoft FrontPage 2000 Keyboard Shortcuts

Keys for Working with Pages

Press	To
Ctrl+N	Create a new page
Ctrl+O	Open a page
Ctrl+K	Create a hyperlink on a page
Ctrl+Shift+B	Preview a page in a Web browser
Ctrl+P	Print a page
Ctrl+ Shift+8	Display non-printing characters
Ctrl+ /	Display HTML tags
F5	Refresh a page
Ctrl+Tab	Switch between open pages
Ctrl+F4	Close a page
Ctrl+S	Save a page
Alt+F4	Quit Microsoft FrontPage
Ctrl+F	Find text on pages or in HTML
Ctrl+H	Replace text on pages or in HTML
F7	Check spelling on a page
Shift+F7	Look up a word in the Thesaurus
Esc	Cancel an action
Ctrl+Z or Alt +Backspace	Undo an action
Ctrl+Y or Shift +Alt+Backspace	Redo or repeat an action

Keys for Formatting Text and Paragraphs

Press	To
Ctrl+Shift+F	Change the font
Ctrl+Shift+P	Change the font size
Ctrl+B	Apply bold formatting
Ctrl+U	Apply an underline
Ctrl+I	Apply italic formatting
Ctrl+Plus Sign	Apply superscript formatting
Ctrl+Minus Sign	Apply subscript formatting
Ctrl+ Shift+C	Copy formatting
Ctrl+Shift+V	Paste formatting
Ctrl+Shift+Z or Ctrl+Spacebar	Remove manual formatting
Ctrl+E	Center a paragraph
Ctrl+L	Left align a paragraph
Ctrl+R	Right align a paragraph
Ctrl+M	Indent a paragraph from the left
Ctrl+Shift+M	Indent a paragraph from the right
Ctrl+Shift+S	Apply a style
Ctrl+Shift+ N	Apply the Normal style
Ctrl+Alt+1	Apply the Heading 1 style
Ctrl+Alt+2	Apply the Heading 2 style
Ctrl+Alt+3	Apply the Heading 3 style
Ctrl+Alt+4	Apply the Heading 4 style
Ctrl+Alt+5	Apply the Heading 5 style
Ctrl+Alt+6	Apply the Heading 6 style
Ctrl+Shift+L	Apply the List style

Keys for Editing and Moving Text and Graphics

Press	To
Backspace space	Delete one character to the left
Delete	Delete one character to the right
Ctrl+Backspace	Delete one word to the left
Ctrl+Delete	Delete one word to the right
Ctrl+X or Shift+Delete	Cut selected text to the clipboard

Keys for Menus and Toolbars

Press	When setting paragraph alignments and indents, to
Shift+F10	Show the shortcut menu
F10	Make the menu bar active
Alt+Spacebar	Show the program icon menu
Down Arrow or Down Arrow (with the menu or submenu displayed)	Select the next or previous command on the menu or submenu
Alt	Close the visible menu and submenu at the same time
Esc	Close the visible menu; or, with a submenu visible, close the submenu only
Ctrl+T	Create an Auto Thumbnail of a selected picture

Press	To
Ctrl+C or Ctrl+Insert	Copy text or graphics
Ctrl+V or Shift+Insert	Paste the clipboard contents
Shift+Enter	Insert a line break

Keys for Programming Applications

Press	To
Alt+F8	Display, edit, or run macros
Shift+Alt+F11	Display the Microsoft Script Editor
Alt+F11	Display the Microsoft Visual Basic Editor

Keys for Help

Press	To
F1	Display the online Help
Shift+F1	Display context-sensitive Help

Keys for Selecting Text and Graphics

Press	To
Shift+Right Arrow	One character to the right
Shift+Left Arrow	One character to the left
Ctrl+Shift+Right Arrow	To the end of a word
Shift+End	To the end of a line
Shift+Home	To the beginning of a line
Shift+Down Arrow	One line down
Shift+Up Arrow	One line up
Ctrl+Shift+Down Arrow	To the end of a paragraph
Ctrl+Shift+Up Arrow	To the beginning of a paragraph
Shift+Page Down	One screen down
Shift+Page Up	One screen up
Ctrl+Alt+Page Down	To the end of a window
Ctrl+Home	To the beginning of a page
Ctrl+End	To the end of a page
Ctrl+A	To include the entire page
Alt+Enter	Display the properties of a selection
Shift+Ctrl+Alt+T	Insert a table
Tab	Select the next cell's contents
Shift+Tab	Select the preceding cell's contents
Hold down Shift and press an arrow key repeatedly	Extend a selection to adjacent cells
Click in the column's top or bottom cell, then hold down Shift and press the Up Arrow or Down Arrow key repeatedly	Select a column

Office 2000 Bibles — 100% of what you need to learn and master the Office 2000 suite

Packed with practical examples and advice, Bibles are the 100% authoritative, comprehensive and solution-filled references you need to learn Microsoft Office 2000 and its applications. Each Office 2000 Bible includes a CD-ROM with time-saving templates, sample documents, power utilities, ISP (MindSpring) and multimedia software, PLUS a fully-searchable electronic version of the book.

BONUS Quick Start

These Office 2000 Bibles come with a FREE 32-page Quick Start book to help you get up and running on the newest Microsoft Office 2000 applications — in less than an hour!

Microsoft® Office 2000 Bible

0-7645-3261-8 • $39.99 US/$56.99 CAN/£36.99 UK

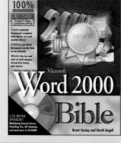

Microsoft® Word 2000 Bible

0-7645-3281-2 • $39.99 US/$56.99 CAN/£36.99 UK

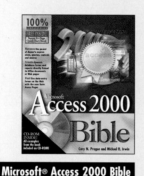

Microsoft® Access 2000 Bible

0-7645-3286-3 • $49.99 US/$69.99 CAN/£42.99 UK

Microsoft® PowerPoint® 2000 Bible

0-7645-3252-9 • $34.99 US/$49.99 CAN/£33.99 UK

Microsoft® Excel 2000 Bible

0-7645-3259-6 • $39.99 US/$56.99 CAN/£36.99 UK

Microsoft® FrontPage® 2000 Bible

0-7645-3313-4 • $39.99 US/$56.99 CAN/£36.99 UK

For more information about Bibles and other IDG Books Worldwide series, visit our Web site at

w w w . i d g b o o k s . c o m

IDG BOOKS WORLDWIDE

Leading the Knowledge Revolution®

Part #D466

Microsoft, PowerPoint, and FrontPage are registered trademarks or trademarks of Microsoft Corporation in the United States and/or other countries. The IDG Books Worldwide logo is a registered trademark under exclusive license to IDG Books Worldwide, Inc., from International Data Group, Inc. Leading the Knowledge Revolution is a registered trademark of IDG Books Worldwide, Inc.

IDG Books Worldwide, Inc.
An International Data Group Company
Foster City, CA 94404

Printed in the USA